GIANTS ALIVE!

By Teresa Jeffries

Modern Curriculum Press
Parsippany, New Jersey

Credits

Photos: All photos ©Pearson Learning unless otherwise noted.
Front cover: Frans Lanting/Minden Pictures. Title page: D. Allen/ Animals Animals. 5:
Frans Lanting/Minden Pictures. 6–7: IFA/Peter Arnold, Inc. 8: Roger De La Harpe/
Animals Animals. 9: Anthony Bannister/Animals Animals. 10: Jeremy Woodhouse/
PhotoDisc, Inc. 11: Johan Elzenga/Tony Stone Images. 12: Colin Prior/Tony Stone
Images. 13: Penny Tweedie/Tony Stone Images. 14–15: Gloria Schlaepfer. 16: E.R.
Degginger/Animals Animals. 17: Paul Freed/Animals Animals. 18: Ted Schiffman/Peter
Arnold, Inc. 19: Roy Toft/Tom Stack & Associates. 20, 21: Joel Sartore. 22: Michele
Westmorland/Tony Stone Images. 23: Manoj Shah/Tony Stone Images. 24: Gerard
Lacz/Animals Animals. 25: Bruce Davidson/Animals Animals. 26: E.R. Degginger/
Color-Pic, Inc. 27: Francois Gohier. 28–29: Doc White/Jeff Foott Productions. 30:
Phillip Colla/Innerspace Visions Photography. 31: Flip Nicklin/Minden Pictures.

Cover and book design by Agatha Jaspon

Modern Curriculum Press
An imprint of Pearson Learning
299 Jefferson Road, P.O. Box 480
Parsippany, NJ 07054–0480

www.pearsonlearning.com

1-800-321-3106

ISBN: 0-7652-1359-1

2 3 4 5 6 7 8 9 10 11 UP 07 06 05 04 03 02 01 00

CONTENTS

To those who care for animals
of all sizes

Chapter 1

Big as an Elephant

How big is big? A giant is very big. In stories, giant people may be taller than trees. Giants in stories are not real. There are real giants on Earth. These giants are animals like the elephant.

◄ African elephant

Giant animals live in different places around the world. The biggest animal that lives on land is the African elephant.

A large elephant may stand over 13 feet tall. That is taller than the top of most rooms. The elephant weighs more than four large pickup trucks.

▲ Herd of elephants

Even the parts of an elephant are big. Its ears are four feet wide. That means an elephant's ear may be as big as you are.

Elephants also have the biggest teeth in the world. Their tusks may be over eight feet long. They weigh up to 80 pounds each.

▲ **Elephant picking leaves**

The elephant's trunk is like a long lip, nose, and hand all in one. The elephant uses its trunk to pick up food. Then the trunk puts the food in the elephant's mouth. The elephant can also drink or spray water with its trunk.

The elephant's nostrils are on the very end of its trunk. When the elephant wants to smell something in the wind, it waves its trunk high in the air.

Mother elephants and their babies live together in herds. An old mother is always the leader. She shows the other elephants where to find water and food.

If there is danger, the mothers make a circle. The baby elephants stand inside the circle where they are safe.

▼ **Elephants bathing in mud**

BIG FACT

Elephants cannot sweat. They like to roll in mud to keep their skin cool.

Chapter 2
Tall as a Giraffe

The giraffe is the tallest animal that lives on land. It stands up to 20 feet tall. The neck is six feet long. You and six friends would have to stand on each other's shoulders to pet a giraffe on the head.

▼ Giraffe

▲ **Giraffe drinking water**

The giraffe's legs are longer than its
neck. This makes it hard for the giraffe to
get a drink. It has to place its front legs
wide so it can reach down to the water.

The giraffe can get some water from
the leaves it eats. It can go for a long
time without having to drink.

The giraffe is always ready to run away from danger. It usually sleeps standing up. When the giraffe runs, it can run fast. If it can't run away, it will kick with its big, heavy feet.

▼ **Giraffes running**

▲ Giraffe eating

When a giraffe stands near trees, it may be hard to see. Its body is covered with big, brown spots. These spots help the giraffe blend in with the tree shadows.

BIG FACT

A lion is the main animal that hunts giraffes. The lion can jump on a giraffe only from a tree or if the giraffe lies down.

Chapter 3
Long as a Python

The biggest snake in the world is the python. It may be over 30 feet long and weigh hundreds of pounds. Even baby pythons are long. When they break out of their eggs, they are already three feet long.

What does a snake this big eat? It eats other animals. A python's jaws can open very wide. Then the python can swallow animals as large or larger than a sheep.

▼ **Children holding python**

A python grabs an animal with its mouth. Then it coils around the animal. The python squeezes until the animal cannot breathe. If a python has a big meal, it does not have to eat for many weeks. It may lie in the sun day after day to keep warm. The warmth helps the snake's body digest the food it has eaten.

▼ Coiled python

▲ Python with eggs

When the mother python lays her eggs, she curls around them. She keeps them warm by shaking her body to make heat.

BIG FACT

The ball python curls up into a ball when someone touches it. The snake's head is in the middle of the ball.

Chapter 4
Up High as a Condor

Birds can be giants, too. The biggest flying bird is the condor. Its wings stretch up to nine feet from tip to tip. It weighs up to 31 pounds.

◄ Condor flying

▲ Condor

The condor's body is covered with black and white feathers. Long, pointed feathers are around its neck. Its head has no feathers. The skin on its head is bright yellow and red.

In the past there were very few condors. Many people were afraid that all the condors would soon be gone.

Some people knew where the last condors lived. They caught two condors. They took care of the birds and helped them with their chicks. Soon they had many condors.

▼ Condors that will be let go in the wild

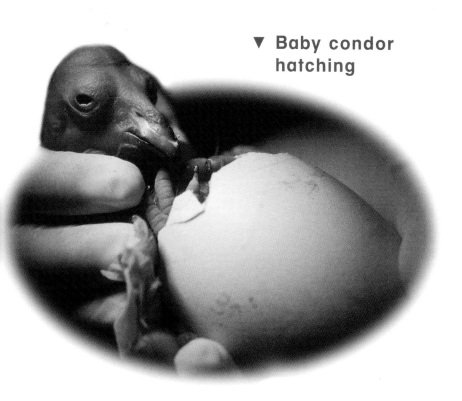

▼ Baby condor
   hatching

The people then let some of the condors go. They tracked the birds to make sure they were safe. Now there are many wild condors again.

BIG FACT

A mother condor lays only one egg every two years.

Chapter 5
Fast as an Ostrich

The largest and tallest bird on the earth is the ostrich. It stands up to nine feet tall and weighs more than 300 pounds.

The ostrich does not look like most other birds. It has a long neck that has no feathers. Its beak is short and wide, and its eyes are very large.

◄ Ostrich

▲ **Ostrich running**

The ostrich can't fly, but it can
run on its long, strong legs. Each foot has
only two toes. If the ostrich is in danger,
it can kick an animal that wants to hurt it.

Ostriches live in groups of 5 to 50 birds. They spend their days looking for plants, bugs, and small animals to eat. Ostriches also watch for danger. They can see an enemy coming from far away.

▼ **Group of ostriches**

The ostrich lays the biggest egg of any bird. This giant egg is about eight inches long and weighs almost four pounds. The eggs are laid in the sand.

The mother and father take turns sitting on the eggs. The mother sits on them all day. The father sits on them all night. When an ostrich is not sitting on eggs, it looks for food.

▲ **Female and male ostrich**

It is easy to tell which bird is the father and which one is the mother. The father has black feathers. Its white tail and wing feathers are long. The mother is gray and brown. Her feathers are not as long.

BIG FACT

Big birds like the ostrich can't fly because their wings are too small and their bodies are too heavy.

Chapter 6
Giant as a Whale

What is the biggest animal that has ever lived? If you guessed the blue whale, you are right. This giant is about 100 feet long. The whale weighs more than 3,000 people all together.

▼ **Blue whale**

Blue whale ▲

Why is this whale called blue? The whale's skin is light gray and white. In the water the skin looks like it is light blue.

As big as the blue whale is, it eats only small fish. The whale swims with its mouth open. As the water goes in, it carries the food in with it.